The Visitor's Guest

Also by Nathan Thompson

the arboretum towards the beginning

The Visitor's Guest

Nathan Thompson

Shearsman Books

Published in the United Kingdom in 2011 by
Shearsman Books Ltd
50 Westons Hill Drive
Emersons Green
Bristol
BS16 7DF

www.shearsman.com

ISBN 978-1-84861-181-8

Acknowledgements

Acknowledgements are due to the following editors and journals, magazines and
e-zines in which versions of some these poems first appeared:

Rupert Loydell at *Stride* and *With*
Alex Davies at *Openned*
Alan Baker at *Litter*
James Davies, Tom Jenks and Scott Thurston at *The Other Room Anthology 3*
David Caddy at *Tears in the Fence*
Rufo Quintavalle at *Nthposition*
Barbara Beck at *Upstairs at Duroc*
Todd Swift at *Eyewear*

Many thanks to Marc Atkins for his generosity and time, for his permission to use
the cover-photograph, and for designing such a stunning cover for *The Visitor's
Guest*. Thanks too to Nick and all at the Curiosity Coffee Shop in Jersey for sharing
my belief that it can take an hour to drink an espresso.

Contents

Looks

Listens

Leans

For Laura

Looks

open book

the ladies were vicious in their requests for flowers

magic is pessimism taken to its logical confusion

discuss

it is getting harder to conclude anything
older than yesterday
                              and even then
excess of confidence can be misleading
'play the scale as if you actually know it
and you'll fool 70% of people' (except musicians)

knowing who's an expert
is perhaps useful for future development
but too many coffees may nonetheless result
in catastrophic diagnoses
about how hearts beat faster when in love with themselves
and everything else is fear

when I left the prefab and came to find you
it was dark in the extreme
alleys of discontent   winter butterflies
fluttered like snow
reversing any sense of control

and I have been inspired to tell you this by a liar
who shudders collages with his broken thumbs
obscuring misprints at pivotal moments in the argument
such that not to go to work is as relevant as
sitting here watching smoke-shards retract into baggy clouds

and when you can say that you can say anything
that was ever concreted under the poetic patio
without the slightest risk
that locks of your hair will become romantic trophies

if I find you agree   I will let you know
that considering these points was important

until then   'mist envelops the whole reckless cathedral'

the thing about

the thing about is
things turn
round a way of seeing

spring colours on an afternoon
is ashes on wednesday by another darker
flowing condensed
or ears' open promise
saved for tomorrow in a frieze of possibilities

now is   continued
flushing out memories
open winter crossed apart too long
from here as
                    lower the windows and
blink perfect days hanging
magic by its own admission

not always guilt   signs and
collective misuse of understanding

shall we go to the

is it worth

before edges focus
kaleidoscope switching

to bleed is   but we're not curious

circulation idea   swap arteries
see what happens
when you come by again veins pantomime dipping

both minds unhurt

now closing the body
tired cushioned mornings

      'I want to stick with you'

little sugar teeth
extract pockets' resistance
grow hungry as light forms
scales balanced   tipping
           waiting

           'love is all in the head'

expressionless feelings dancing hard
splits of crows dribble the skyline
figured confusion
                being intense
to lick lyric dry
folk-sung under summer blankets

securely visual

somewhere is a body carrying the psychological baggage of sleepless nights

I follow you under your eyes folding tattooed skin   recycling aesthetics
until no bigger than a red letter

days spent in foreign language   wet with blood held up on docked
fingers counting institutions trashed and toxic

driving   a drunk in a memory of driving

painted on a sunday

late   sees only
changing spaces

the park is playing with
your mind as

what are you reading
is it good

music turns three paces inward
weighted against a blank page

bliss is   to pass up tenses
quills or feathers   equally you

airbrushed

appeals to loneliness   lost contours
the sea falling far away

could this be any more romantic
                    'stuff happens'   more or less
as blossom downs obscuring vision with a kaleidoscope
over each eye

patterns ratcheting

                    paintings of relationships

                                      technically very beautiful

news from the hill

getting the sun always right   fluctuations
it is noon-time in the tropics
                                        here it is
almost intimate   half light differentiating
love from lovers in a bare room

the children sleep   mountains dance
refusing any move to point up
towards moments seen through indifference

the moon on the other hand is very high   imagining something
other than what it already is   an obsessive
diet of cow juice chugging its dim engines
over a horizon of hurt professors

this is our twenty-eight days to three six five
wandering through a hall of mirrors

as though to pass the same street a thousand times
seems the real thing   you didn't see him / her
also comparing simple

angels

there are as many fingers as there are
owls in heaven
                remember   the world is holding the keys
to your heart and making a big mess of it
THIS / DOES / NOT / WORK   written on each chamber

by implication there are not enough owls in hell
because the remainder are in purgatory today
knitting ladders
                unusual   as they seem
to fly so naturally you could touch the way they fly

is it ever not autobiographical   'the key to your castle?'
I accept there could be some confusion here

back in the picture some houseflies join me
in what has become known as *the post-ultimate glade*
where we feed on meat and other flies
things left behind by crunchy feathers
'life on earth as we know it in the rain'

okay I'm flagging   I'll write this story   in terms
I try to relax no part of you that aches
with emotional complexity
                      the moon
giant and yawning on an impressive table

but something is yet lacking   handing us back
autonomy   too intimate   vague enough
for a doctor at midnight who signs for his alter ego
all my life I've been in love with its colour on my lips
as if drunk boys stomp on secretive shoulders
then commute nervously admitting to all the taints that look good
motionless as statues of ushers selling oranges
in pictures of old thought themselves into part   past cities
without recourse to method

                     do you have any questions

try praying or turning to the noise under a cow when its bell rings
time almost as beautiful as she lives and carries
a stetson for the richest disease in the room
full of people I love just as one moment becomes
not quite the next   or the wing I reject as
absolutely false   an established compendium of nails
down a blackboard placed in me by nature

to recap   *I begin the establishment of the castle*

the bare minimum   trusting your name
that is to say others need pay no further
attention to crawl through the grass with me
water flowing underneath where the moat . . .

flesh alone has escaped reclining bones
regurgitated through the beak   'appeals?'   or
     screaming monotone dialectics emphatic carolling

these words are too dense   I prefer the way
you snuck out of the dormitory 35 times
20 losses poking holes in your armour

the rest of the evening passes
medication reduced to architecture
crumbling beneath your feet

you called to say you were dead
your one and only   the prophet's hair
flowing from his unwritten turret

ivy   where   is suitable for perching
dancing even   the distance after that   owls are so wise

I thought to myself that this must be god

courting the days

can you promise winter is shadows

I have consulted the philosophers and agree

less is more when it comes to movement

on the basis of the stars

                      we build a bridge

then burning talk of lips half open

brief histories

1

have you
have you finished
your balance is

2

did I move
just for a second the music
ultra violet
                    tastes

3

was it
was it equal to
discussion
                    you say

4

how stone
over time
keeps lids open
                    coins gather

5

are you
are you gnomic
point out
                toenails removed bell-shaped

6

would concentrate
affect outcome
milk confrontation
                        high moon cocked wrong story

7

who is
who is looking for
stop that noise

offshore lifeboat

all entwined
words whirr and flow
from eye to eye

music below speech
an effect of the medium
engraved with a blue knife

at precisely eleven
we fall silent
swaying in unison

add an hour
onto a dream of poppies
communing with the dead

this for serious profit
now the return
perhaps   it's worth it

offshore is safe   bombproof
to wounded sensibilities   occupation
for you   these nasdaq love-songs

nightfall in the colonies

the court is assembled

we've spoken of too many things now
to believe in anything
                          'he's been trying to sort our accounts for a year'

    whisper

under a blue lamp your hands appear as eyes
wrapped round an excursion   stuck in traffic
it is gloomy but precise
                          rain falls (as usual) on the central reservation

    where am I

I have learned to trust what you mean when you say the word
                          'language'

some things occur naturally but not this   'is remembrance
always on sunday?'   guilty to only
half-answer your questions   I didn't notice days passing
down into water   vortex full-lipped as a freudian dream

it seems we are no longer authorised to bid for survival
a long white hat covers everything like snow
flopped over a lumpy mountain   cemeteries pocked
with miniature falls prop your card table
surrounded by toothless mummies   *j'accuse*   children
picking up their parents
                          this is one of

    page turns

poultice to closure   mumbling a ledger
mist outside these grand buildings   distilled from
earlier thoughts
                    'when they say twelve men
do they remember thirteen was intended?'

warehouses close to tears   a face at a broken window
insults its image
                    beyond your distance   towards the rails

the magic study of happiness

following your example   tomorrow
I brighten like flowers opening a book
with the discovery of more flowers

                colours to play
in the general direction of being in love accidentally
cooling anemones in rock-pools   we have lived
yesterdays beside an ocean   following the creek
on sunny mornings

          should I be writing this for you
I'm not sure   some gifts are unwanted but

to see summer from a broad perspective of winter
big things held in your retina

            mill ponds where
white elephants swish off a dusty day
emerging bright stars at an appropriate distance

I imitate you like a train of shadows
like a cat pulling backwards on its lead
like   'the angel knows everything   every second counts
fasten your seatbelt   we're leaving'

here are all the vines entangled
when a ray of light moves me
I will expire on the moss

to fail to learn would be   emphatic
   'if only I had ancestors   I would make gold and your remedies'

wishes entering a land

it's dark again   and there are things
we haven't said   really necessary
a skeleton in a pale suit doffing his hat
smiling as only the dead know how
('lord of the heavy sentence')
I've left my compass behind and ~~I want to cry~~

having to be like that   a performance
under the whole sky for a couple of people
frozen solid in their beds   unblossoming
bulbs which flower not blossom anyway
as jasmine stirs its cold around the door
ignorant of nothing   ever really opening

~~lyrical place~~   disaster suffers thought
demanding money I can't give
through the medium of envelopes but
lend me your hand and we'll talk the ridges
down from a high desert at morning our breath
hoping lizards won't come in and ruin it all

stone faces erect words by a frozen lake
back bent for remuneration   'move away'
if you can I don't know how to tender / end this
but will meet someone soon who sees
a policeman through fog twirling his moustache
to spin the stars a record set straight

the machine arrives

your argument   flesh
colossal woods migrating
slowly
          fields in which to put things
at what volume   are you set

I love the shape of fibres
as they move beyond the back page
shading why we can't be said between four walls

you create your own logic and stick to it
soon it will be snowing   all this and have forgotten petals

houses

stay close   this evening's ~~tender~~ ending
so many words to describe the same
moonlight falling asleep in an eye

am I telling you too much   perhaps
you will not want to see me
after this marches off into the distance
leaning wide out of the window
as if after a cigarette

I want to be close (as I've said)
gasping prior to your softness but
what was never meant to be illicit
is here in the country washing clean
in streams intended for consciousness
white noise   a pirouette

evening poster girl

light and sky   *exhibit A*   and only
do not fold   the world is turning
colourful as we speak of the day's news
passing us messages in whispers

if I had something less jumpy for you
this would be it   introversion
fobbed off a watch clocking the hours
as they pace between your cloven eyes
but no   dark lashes are all the tomorrows of interrogation
we need   and this is
                                        something
opened out like a newspaper on the ocean
images more important than words
coded beyond recognition of you   us
a parliament of owls asking questions
each wish cloned into last sunlight   aerated

noctivigation for beginners

the way you find   or me
checking the range of darkness as it falls
concentration on objects   how they reappear
relevant in morning
                                    to think through
is always slightly tomorrow   altered
at the first hurdle of worship

we are talking in undiscovered tenses
other ways to look up and note shocked welts
painfully move slowly

except for birds flying over
almost silently   twisting paths to another wet lung

ellipses for painters

when you think you have a question
what colour is it

word of mouth
glitzed on the lawn   open brackets   why is
where empty becomes

a godly oath thought too little

on my account   how is it   'that'
we watch   rather than swear on
extravagantly   your charms

scarcely relevant

the art of heart is pure politics

reversed left and right

hit head   sensory browser is delighted

autonomy against a world of money and power

life rafts verbally   fish stocks decline

wet faces for the sponged clergy

'fate can be conical'   interswapped

moments in time necessarily redundant

twice over   under a yew tree

me standing   simply satirical

snipped up   consistently effaced

every facet has its shadow

cold walls   'imagine'   passes by
networked with your one heart-beat
taking a pull at a mirror
'listen to the echo'
                        is this why
loving you   touching the night
brings down houses   makes this chain
of events seem natural
                              to meet you
composing a symphony under scented roses
in the beer garden   'here is the point'
dark   low voltage   unnatural speech

dances with conversable provision

and mutter in chains
changing matter

        what
        so long as secret
        held gaze
        continuing

touch paper
for pauper's torch

        how
        to remedy this
        without
        further murmurs

the sky is getting darker rain flicks / mistake / litters matches on rooftops
can't stand up in here without threatening

             the ~~veiled~~ eye works its magic
             we are all quite [quite] happy

Listens

lay by maria

when murder is the music of a night's soft opening
capital   dreams further interrupted   stop
high ranking raising spectres
                              dead spies swapped
casual conversation focus slinking ideologies
disputes stirred a la mode
                        slipping down
easily virtuous in holiday modal inversions

cross or forehead newspaper certainties
hide out in the woods endlessly fucked
razed ground as if zero importance tolerance

this focus bickers beautiful   as if
                                  as if
                                  as if
can I complete the evening's news

conference opening papers   is this what 'opening'
three tunes have I stolen   impersonations sexology carved
brains into new shapes for disdain
frequency broadcasting medicine island
new season mislaid hinted at cancelled virgin
high concept low brow strike iron or
minor gold's repeated riff on our own

expanded slightly   I just
                                            I just
                                          I just
bad joke cap and bells three sets one window
transformation seen through black without saying

the visitor's guest

presentiment by parts

ornament
                    lived russian doll-like
eventually revealing nothing
smaller   continuation and
to speak   things change irrevocably
never recognise
                              balance
bring home the way white blouses conceal
picture primitive chance encounters dictated

what's about to happen so secrets believe

*

did you cry as forms alter
unreported agendas
                                          milk
                              dust
                    table
          inquisitive

to belong   parallel paper thin lines
sloped opportunities under pushed requirements
commit to hold
                    parliament of circles
intertwined compasses trip spun four corners follow painting
sea legs the sofa that loves you non-semantic language analogues
and your friends the toads their first geography
pages in chains embracing

                    well to yes I think

hidden aesthetics run through us like unwanted transactions

*

~~but the small cool room~~
~~vents building too otherwise quiet~~
~~jumps association~~
                         ~~itself elastic~~
~~tired as if edited~~
~~bounced confinement~~
~~passacaglia for solo violin~~

'next to the lifeless things follow those which partake a growing life and
then a feeling'

world wide lock jaw whole finger up staggering

*

the conversation fox planteth his dwelling in the steep cliffs by the seaside
ransacketh every corner of his wily sconce   his noble stumps
quit his coat from their jaws

	beasts of venery	
	their case:	*martens*
		squirrels
		badgers
		otters
		foxes
	for skin and flesh:	*hares*
		conies
		deers
		foxes

tell me if I lie
        so full of windings
        to disseize this their espial

the mire of his tail against their eyes in lieu
gives the fico: *to siege*
                      "force
                      "mine
                      "sword
                      "assault
                      "famine

                              the start of the way
                              attempt against him

*

preferring gain to delight

making gain delight

precedent   deer leap over the pale
                 tin moon honoured with silver pennies

where we are   the otherness of world
performing nature   decadent bodies
art fingered blooming

                          pyres of broken mirrors
make argument   disappearing destroyed
sentiment long for you as frail night sharpens
not being there at all inside form   shadow
honesties once authorised populated facts

I would like to introduce 'the map's escalation'
lairs where threaten uneasy true words winning
with thinking to bring you news
pared down   good themselves the wrong
~~tragic~~ charts probe imaginations
what passes for found there
          baseless destructive enthusiasm
                              but to outcome
<u>nonaesthetic</u>   unchecked in costume reason
a similar pattern to   I love you
                              romantic independent
swum through backwards   needy   simple enough hearts
minded tragic   parataxis   military order assumed secular force
related runs in an apposite direction
                              that entrance is a fact
                              that exit is a true
                              that roots like towers
                              that were once governments

world making lived life small scale and only cry
to play it from within tied sacred while we move the edge
I wish I knew
          but always ~~and always~~

*

this language will sour what the tongue touches

*

~~rubbish~~ to make these demands is dead
the party winding up now thoughts have their hats
on vagrant colours harm caused
smoking behaviour in elegantly turned phrases
but what it forms not lips contrast sensual
the casual scarf look farewell echoes of
commercials ruthless as hang over aspiring

here's a saying worth useless touches
manipulation how you mutate loving
to courtesy more than sufficient
doorbell advocates running laughing
actual things imaginary
little aliens
           spoonfed
speak ~~english~~ no this won't pass you
salt wounded add injury to perjury
each trial wholly encouraging
                    the same
                  basic ~~sour~~
goodness knows expression prolonged photographic
makes each
        inasmuch
             a point of entry

      radical

          as an adult

    as a late

        like a whole

            subsides

percentage of did not answer

undertow nocturnal focus
waves groups leaving one by one
unproductive arc to resuscitation

my love these are animal days oblique
sensation close to but
kind of understanding

why you're out there deeply imbricated
drawing lines back into nature
economic – *flash* – ecology

then propped under streets
highways vicious turgidly
capture no more than I do

non-delivery probably accounts
characters out of setting
processes mutability

but for can assume changes / people
fear / life as solid subject
that passage about the neighbours

now and at the hour

standing up are you ~~drama~~ begun to retaliate
left blues and blacks painted on sirens

> you're supposed
> I thought we could

taken from behind liverish prejudice
the walk is newsworthy protest used to be songs
knocked out in a few minutes no *love* anymore
perfume copper flavour to intestines
you did not have

> dying eventually so no problem fists
preach don't too much fits up ciphers unintelligible
> 'we have to hurt sometimes'

now to bite face back muzzled numberless
reasons prosecution is illegal
migrating in circles

> yellow rain washes double
> lines cordoned / condoned
> put on prohibited identification
> ~~tea of course that's homely~~

still someone as mouth O forms
along now nothing to say here

g
e
n
u
i
n
e

b
l
a
n
k   but whistle

perhaps take pictures
notes down clear pass baton to next payment run
relay information no big bother
is watching wide-screen white noise nothing
information blackout wash same
or is a dog-lover [bitch-fucker style] as he observes
how not screaming is captured
heaving weight under bottles ironic if not so
inexcuse X 2 or number please
        number please
        <u>number</u> <u>please</u>
        who you [~~gonna~~] call

hearts just burst sometimes ~~sir~~
information you should know ~~sir~~

    blue kisses
    smile on
retelling knife song only later
left out excises return investigation rigor
26 separate new wounds do the double
more than man's laughter all but in the building bent passes coins
hooks to place things ferociously progressive over eyelids
        'blue knives'   a year at sea

can you this [political] without straying
praxis love is fine save where understands <u>love is hot</u>
tears when you get home what say you children and
I don't know this but trust to whatever
god-like birds circle bald-headed or wig-hidden
to protect and defend / against
                             simple things
such as honesty breeding crocodiles in weeping sewers
you think rain will come down clean
acid burn-out   shelter
        ~~shelter~~ me
        from curious
        burrowing   like a
                 [like a]
                 ~~like a~~
licked wound back beat up on
this will not stop until just ~~search~~
stop and
think and   search
on down on repetition

to refuse this growth as are
throwing votes in glass houses
back together again like bottles
back to
              what remember from this
cannot put return / delete / return
crossings out nylon tight balaclava
head gear always
criminal there's got to be otherwise lost but no
words will never [~~nothing~~] happen
don't to be buried what we say
happened
happened ~~sir~~
reach out long barrow maria lost

morning series parallel

when questions asked how personal
trained edge of the middle ground
age we have associated our associates
beautiful bedtime with cartography
sheets your contours breathing

lying the lyric pores popping shaved
slick blood speculation specification lipid
movement limpid colour combination unread
at twilight love is elastic
displaced atomic searching its nucleus

parliament of owls [passport
music an elegant table laid
bare blue as reflection] winks distorted
mirror toning / identity pill
cards upturned the final moment

how the script was used

bleak front
                west bound
we are solar today   northern lights
so to depend on the compass
moral certitude
                        yes you are right to question
wind blows where most to seek it
plain talking low and whistle tumble
down the barrel of a gun fists raised
finger twitch
                queen of minimal movement
the bed scarcely whispers as it blushes

today we are found wanting everything
sunrise satellites down infrastructure burnt out
each slickly tuned beginning apocalyptic rhetoric
laughing silently behind your hand

praise indefinite at the second altar murmured compromise
misleading transports into enclosure feeling
the white room turning
                        inside away
on the ranges flint for wicked thoughts

you who have believed everything
~~splendid~~   the rest wracked over our own
embers' twilight shoot-out now triangulates
ideas of east
                space time travelling
a coat made
many colours so long as it's cheroot brown

so into a corner migrate south
to take the waters

                        princess love and hearts
extends come downs from her tree   trip wire
promoted in one eye moment   we to rip at home strip bark
whip orders earl grey and think of her

an aquarium for michael tippett

in this year   water-gardening
a flattened seventh
                        episodes of corpus christi
my heart is all on flood   delay following
skin-tight   untouched
                         why 'in this year?'

as if   chronicles of sudden movement
fixed in time vertically
                     but you know that already
with every nearly raised finger
broken to praise and bless

I am sorry to grieve you
falling from the fountain
                     implied utterance
pumped up always to downward

these are methods for avoidance
at the still centre   bubbling below
enquiries into two sides of the river
feeding a remnant that escaped
                       'the boy and the lady'
restored to an age when little was attempted beyond
the registration of fact

        some of them were blinded
        some of them were banished
        so all traitors were laid low

who tells this now
hangs burning things on their feet
hawking at gnats

but I've come away with categorical paces
far from you   pirated   indexical   sad
liquid eyes rented from others
comatose on private health
copyright difficulties surmounted
hard cash drowning blinds and buildings

estate agents on the lash let loose through a city of
dreadful light doctored unsafe by stashed retainers
crossing over lips with stitches lipo-sucked
corny   a kiss for the cameras   skim-flick
freshly filtered coffee as you flutter the door

you risked everything for a white canvas
walled up
                    left in style
                                        cut down   glazed
                                                            star

travelling suitable
     cloud flesh
condensing speed of words
orchestrated

                    legs
floral echoing on their axis

this is an experiment in seeing
figures as faces red-eyed
ash on a card table
                                        wingless
concerns in glass dishes
x-rayed beyond recognition

                              scope for
micro-change as imported skin
tears   broken where they fall

I'll tell you again in slow emotion
mood-lit from beneath torched comfort

                'this is the way the mirror flows'

dr x leans over the couch   *so many*
recumbent stylites

                        seen through a grill

daily imaginings
                        psychotropes
persuaded to divination

he writes his thoughts on the wall
then erases them

~~dream study 1~~

~~through forests north of the amazon~~
~~what changes~~
                ~~upper waters of the rio alto trombetas~~

~~an eerie morass   projected ideas~~
~~stretched as far as evil~~
                        ~~fruit hanging motionless~~
~~grey expanse of water~~

~~small holes and cracks begin to appear in the sides~~
~~letting in facts~~

* * *

~~ds 2 + notes to a cure~~

~~morning   broken~~
~~heavy~~
              ~~water~~
~~negates   faces at windows~~
~~looking out~~

                                        ~~where~~

~~looking~~————————————————————————~~acrid~~
~~in~~—————————————————————————————~~rain~~

          ~~'can you bring yourself to say it?'~~

* * *

~~ds 3~~

~~we leave~~
            ——————~~prewritten~~
            ——————~~text~~
            ——————~~translucent~~
            ——————~~pearls~~
            ——————~~distorted~~
~~every direction but home~~

* * *

these sassy sunflowers bagged for market

attendant creatures
                         opening dialogue
where double concertos undulate over cornfields

are we in the town or the country

whose dances are these

if we can no longer turn to each other
synchronised   divided into two tenements
intersecting   we are silent
            enemies under a tassled lampshade
facing away into the dark unreachably
as baby noises
                         in upper rooms which lie
to the edge of text

more to the night
                         of other flowers
moon opening   louche
on a lecherous voyage
                         I had forgotten
today was a marker   clear answers given
another year   shivering knees at an altar

behind trust   except in   itself
                                   myself
                                   dare I say it

this tawdry episode brings us briefly
to our collateral love
                            dropping questions
in a library not mentioned in the law suit
            'a naughty house   all uncleanliness there'

the rest bombed out   dark and dirty
morsels of evidence for other worlds
having strength to replicate
                        evidence
                        against said parties
                        intimate first met
                        approaching conversion

the story   such as it can be reconstructed
is as follows

ultraviolet   chlorophyll   sex   a famous painting

through music we escape across the city
water phasing out in mist

I walk the sign again in retrograde
doing things I shouldn't
                            refusing
to even own a dog to carry on the escalator
starred with righteous madness

other theories also have a number of supporters

the slow movement takes slightly less than 26,000 years
to dissolve completely through church bells
burgeoning outer suburbs   industrial areas
holy   orbs of influence
                                        elevation in status
moral over capital definition   rebels   mental diseases
nervous disorders   astrologers

            traditionally this rotation is calibrated
by butterfly wings clustered
between business-class mankind and irresolution
experienced before it arrives
                              but today
indecent symbols itch the skin of a new tattooee
at the vernal equinox
                        'you need to maintain a compassionate heart'

I arrive with negative connotations at inner fulfilment
floating out on a tide affected by fervour for war
without ever understanding it

pretext   somebody was needed to turn the pages
            of the esteemed dane rudhyar
            pacifist
            first space probe among equals

            starting from the star '0'
            assumes a platonic month of 2143 years without oxygen
            until AD2154
                              a date
            known to be somewhat arbitrary

I
     cannot tell
          in a pathless land
how home is

the meridian of this first star
          cup raised

    [*the age will generate individual water carriers*]

multiples of O

how shall we enter the terms themselves conditional
hot rocks on a dead eye red with morning
open book teeth dusty ephemeral destitution
collated returned unedited how a feeling looks
elbow in face outside you say what
rubbery buttocks on the idea of seed
yellow fields bruised with smoking
stone circles empty each the same perceived
cast before meaning melted from abortion
zygote qualified too much explained by

there has to be conducted steel water tight experiments
electricity snuck through whiskey beliefs expensive
you will not divorce transubstantiate argue
child turns child to stone withers on alternative
gospel magazine rack hieroglyphics
agreed casket credit debit we can afford
until tomorrow to be happy bishop-like
or at diagonals to alternatives playing
lucky in the wrong game planned cuts
planed away double helix the same
as love spread out sickly operations
silence sounding what we have let down
across the rain rubbed diamonds
across the what dubbed what

I really am yes / yes if not
not worse remind me
concerning misplaced marble
tables scrubbed increasing
turning roll awake major umbilical
cadence out weeps unconfirmed anaesthetic

Leans

spatial practices

beneath the haze
a wave of verticals

this is a very old story
part three at the opera
momentarily arrested by vision
distance composed through mother of pearl

quietly the romance of a phantom   paths that correspond
paroxysmal places in monumental reliefs

a park in the dark reads in it
the universe that is constantly exploding
its giant rhetoric of excess   mystical textures

next time   to be you

would you, but would you

attempting the traditional   or rather
outbreaks of houses in the face of violence

the way my father talks of cable street
as if it's not there and it isn't
columbia road a jumble of murder and high flowers
days to be gone back to among many

there is a hint that this is a set up
but to what   how can I be sure
that I'm not just queuing   throwing cobbles
at advancement

but you   would you deceive me
with a coalition of the lost
forgetful of fighting meaning
until pistachio husks litter tasteless pavements

you will understand now why I wear camouflage trousers
as I walk the streets   a man in a folksong
so-called because rain fell on us all
peripheries eaten like knots in a wooden bicycle
     if I could only taste the things you consider to be abstract
     somebody might just understand
               dreams are about
as constant as it gets under off-violet footsteps

we bled here
and sank our teeth into whatever was going
long before taking highgate
           or richmond park green
conducting chaotic rites under each streetlamp as it lit
the best of science and religion

having confidence
it is difficult to assume the necessary posture
out of white teeth to lick what's mine

night drew on   let's take a ride
bringing loan-wigs out of bright-eyed crevices
transitional passages mobile and wet underfoot
as long-haired kitten-slippers
        'locomotion in a foreign land'

I want to take you home   but
you are lying in the snow erotically
breathing   smoke   slipping down
your open blouse
          stop before
too much is revealed   nettles sting
corked wine in a tired city   dully

and before we slip away into separateness
remember it was intended such an alliance
would milk the old ways dry
as water slaps the inner sanctum
defences down and out   upon the shore
rest   limbs   creeping to rainbow lights
in a doorway
        71 quilter street
songs wrung lost   I believe her name was

last accounts misleading

translating hope street

night   heat lifts   (of course)   we are supposed
to be singing   you
                  empty pentagrams
italicise squares [piazzas]   a brazen head
born 1665   reborn   here   not too far
but   enough
              a clump of pine
tightly compressed   *poor child*   potential

warm and sweet smelling   an island in a river
'everyone looks like a murderer'
maybe it's the cape
              fangs   turning
through a glass of wine   big awkward leaves
behind an obscene idea in frosted mirrors   red lit
a buyers' market   shaping each other's
dance to swarming rosebuds   shadows opened for tomorrow to fill

the visitors adrift

the price of distance is unique
back of jacket   an era in your private madhouse
researched and humane
                              smoothly written   dense

tomorrow we are going away and you are frightened
leaves will fall without you   eaten whole
the cure is to think that night is closing in
everywhere over the moon and stars may be untrue
making their way on a procession of crutches

these lives have been a long time gawping
through presences   the imperial war museum
a vortex upending somewhere at sea propeller driven

the world's oldest psychiatric hospital
in cockney slang is   1247's many
parallels   *abdh*   for some reason
magical   aleister crowley dispersed
into little portions of colin wilson
pennies dropped through lists of names
clanging in a belfry stolen from popular song

your eyes are bright   tearful at the thought
of roast mouse giving money to your father

at present we are richly anecdotal
this is here   small island   money
and there
                    now here   the age of determined reformers
propping up solutions in bunhill   aldermen riding
from shoreditch back to tomorrow
countries that would do anything to make her smile

some of her sister's deluded subjects
lie naked in the half light of a winter afternoon
forgotten pleasantries for tourists   trading lewd remarks
in the straw
                    'I have created you masks for your sorrow'

an unsettling calm   hot black desolation
undertakers down the road   m&r meats
but who   gentle angel   a mirror for crying
cheap turned wings in the red lion   intimate
fantasies about growing old in gutter moss
believing in more things than the play
between footfall and home
                                        this is about
the course of an apparently normal evening
hung out on a wire   skull to skull
mature trees slow on an avenue in the afternoon
that   before   songs emerging from
peanut shells dropped to the floor
written on an old typewriter
                                        split hands remain
loved on a yellow ceiling patterned with theatrical gestures
here is here   seen through the bent glass of our laboratory hotel

* * *

your postcard became small propped upright on
the piano   setting an atmosphere for gangsters
each time one walked by
                        the tiny toad
jimmy the map   no-handed sue

even as a baize table upturns on splintered
hands   the game goes on

(crows shocking worms to attention
my shoes softening to melted tarmac)

     an appreciation of distance spells hours
     brailled out for audio only
                       your soft voice
       hummed twilight   if all songs were
     hard to speak   what then
     learning bicycle tricks in stop motion animation
     ringing a bell with your teeth

question everything   question the lights
written in words that fall on your doormat unpaid
I don't really need to tell you   if you've got this far
we've probably already spoken   and   you remember
staining glass during that interlude before the reformation
arcade machines taught how to brighten with a human touch
to hold   gamble   roll   and play again
for increasing stakes fed to the dogs
a slow jazz number I think
old-fashioned patterns with recycled sawdust
          'you just find yourself in these places
when you are asleep at home'   a way of being
ten years younger than you're trying to get away with

kick me to get your attention

* * *

reduced noise levels in the beer garden
after eleven pm   a major government directive
un-appealed

       'to the residents of islington

I need you to stay behind   I didn't even know you
were in my bed'   fishing for compliments
getting   rain blessing trees
outside your open window   piano sounds again
prepared against the backdrop of a black mountain's
imagined seriousness
                              here we are or were
important   nostalgia   sentiments to re-inhabit
religiously forgotten   replaced with double-glazing
propping up the bar   'old mistakes are so pretty'
     a picture about   a play
for   mystery denizens of the 19th century

* * *

autumn hits beautiful with a googly punch
drunk leaves falling   digital jabber
passing this morning   windows broken
angels out of live television
crumble light on rain
                              mozart in a café
scribbling myths on his backwards-facing mask
for others to dance with dolly parton at the rodeo
of a victorian-style christmas brought closer
wreathed in spoken smoke   cakes from the museum
to tender bankers   upward-gliding scholars
pure voices for the historically uninformed
over croissants in the canteen library
quills out   pinching inches given vertical
miles from anywhere circling blades for upturned
criminals
                    sighs of a bed on a spiral staircase   iron ready
sheets   tomorrow's replacement

* * *

every time we walk in your direction music happens
tin pan alley   having a coke with
hearts that are true but to what daily
inattention   a cartoon buried under rubble
meeting matches   sparks up conversation
inspiration for three and a half minutes   'brightly coloured
croaking'   no space to move
without encountering   still young

I am burrowing under water   touched by its rays
until we are nowhere   presences
in london's biggest saxophone showroom
more expressive than faces your car drove down
those stairs at a clatter   bobbing eight minutes off the surface

roll to the centre   a peaked assembly of towers
then back to your party   parting hair
differently   splitting into nights
of love realised   homeless beauty kissing to be tricked
two four six nine   thieves under old names
I called you before the plump of my belly
that bounces off your ivory   sales and repairs
upriver   glass dancing   helping people
with their thoughts blanked in the street
by loved ones   'features are getting smaller
even jockeys'   ambitious exploration and studies
of form   sofas with no clothes on
full of politics and gender framed by domestic
unknown species gravitating towards
sleep broken   trying rain on nautical charts
docked between zurich and london by the corner

* * *

huge trees   along old street
argos   a deep well punctuated by rumblings
punk wine style   you sing angelically
shirt-sleeves dipped in bleach until inside
arms fall off leaving ghosts of wings
filmed by a soldier   'domestos was a deterrent
in the roman army'   leaving architects
wasted unable to dance
                              the new walk
temple paintings   emergency but nothing's broken
second-hand handshakes down broken glass alley
bits flecked in your heart
methamphetamine
attack
he lost all his toes
must increase

* * *

the deed producing heartache
attention focussed   setting ghosts walking
'nobody survived'   harsh landscape
sparingly and beautifully time-travelled
uncorrupted by sin   a slice of sweetest
feeling   dislocation
                              inveigle or be
inveigled   quacks   magical philtres and receipts
occult notes   whips   furs   bankers
physicians   confessors   tricks and subtleties
                   'but since I knew what was coming next
                   we'll paint on the walls the true
                   identity of jack the ripper…'

* * *

'less is more'   made from street litter
emerges centre stage through your open window
urban detritus   conceptual rigour
flowing into   'the sea is very far away
a minority of people being discarded'
everything from his car to his passport
burns in an expanded field

                              thirst quenched
any art that isn't painting   you'll be here soon
I could be happy and confident you know
reworked after a battering during casting
at the foundry   mannequins destroyed
junk plastic to expand   seemingly weightless
with mystical and religious   arcana
rained on pudding lane   rich presuming knowledge
a monument to protect it from flames and zechariah
lifting his eyes from the indestructible city
a prisoner laughing on his island determined
by sacred geometry measuring out a plan

* * *

it's hard to leave without your eyes
jars of flowers outside bunhill   ponytail
hair up   red   apocalipstick smile
you're all doomed you bastards
artists' books   days of wine and
who fall in love with her   tight under
racks of emotion
                         I point to furious
clouds outside the shop   foreign
exchange students dancing together
shadows of an oak tree
                              it's all

pretty exciting   your new world map
waiting to take showers or a massage
for a list of words

    shy
    steam
    athletic
    everywhere
    horror-porn
    see
        you
            again
    hardly
    communicate

he has the time of his life
friendly   gothic
a museum to love
after a not so funny joke

as soon as it is sunny out
in the park / cemetery
it is not safe for me there

* * *

in the index   still   from 'garden state'
where everything ends   I'm not back yet
but not to leave here would be   finished
'museum dress'   again   *URGENT   looking
for someone to sing the alphabet at my funeral*
                                phoebe cates   who is you
who I think is gorgeous   moves so over the sea
'designated most likely to be arrested'

an exhibition for   the provinces
islands asleep   time   how to spend the night

the piper

clearing your throat   here's music
the rest of our town has fallen ill
three or four women with high crowned hats
write the introduction to a riff on dancing

not a time to be cruel

founded neither on religion or prudence
you lit a cigarette
                    chewing garlic I asked
but who here ordered hats

wind blows through leaves like remorseless courage
directing many (I forget their names)
and order is restored   do re mi
                     only five years
                     dead-carts
                     after these events took place

that knows and so do I

since this evening has failed I go
quiet by the fire between scents of dog-roses and light
tremolos on a flute I worshipped because you played it

how do you untangle such
                              things
tiny bells and footsteps taken into a photograph
of the way radio-waves used to swing before fading

this tune is contagious   or at least
woven from the texts of a hundred flowers
at the v&a   'we should visit'

but outside it is cold and fear is the new black
cloaked in focussed tropes zeroed by the same
hundred poets still dressed as flowers

I've inked you in a drink will you join me

this is the way whispers start
striking matches   briefly smiled in at the window

black butter she said

of the extant
explaining that there are similarities
used as an aphrodisiac
                              dried toads
lulled in a storm   from the far distance
high on his cup   the captain asks
and his deep resonant voice founders
painted on walls by his countrymen

'all my riches shall be yours'

his sons in fury laid an ambush
taxed it with eels and sundry futures
tending towards the bilingual

                                     I work here
killing nor consenting thereto   incapable of
                                     transacting legal business
                                     hear me out

here   me   out   free of ransom

for the return of your castle   setting
a boy to whistle a warning   sun
casting doubt would lead   to perpetual peace

words   send him scurrying home   at midnight

telling the story   how
                              afraid to peep out
a shadowy black figure sacrificed a knuckle
in service to his master

if you're such a bad girl I'll send for marie tourgis

while bailiffs gad about the island so covered
by lice it is impossible to see clothes beneath

          cord
          wrapped round your neck twice

le loup garou   shape changer
for two cabots of wheat   crouches

at the foot of st paul ascending
quartzed rose attended by lucifer's cats

          a place of pilgrimage as soon

as night was sufficiently advanced
knocking at a door of gold and silver

the robbers then made for bouley bay
trustynge in your fidelities   a storm ringing from the deep
one cabot of rye three sols for an obit

          never written on the rim of an
                  upturned chalice

left in the hands of strangers

it was slow work

money was not plentiful

a lady had lost a valuable ring

entering his darkened room on tiptoe

          'when he touches it the cock
                  shall crow'

at six o'clock the next morning
in the hearth too little is worth nothing
and that little is too much   torn from his flesh with combs
          we are apart a bird

flying in at the door

dawn breaking
'you know the price by now sir'   whose journey is always anti-
                                                                            clockwise

approaching dark

this is the alchemical secret   turning base flesh
gold to touch
back down the hill to wolf's cave
where pirates or cold fish will greet you   with a kiss
                                                               in the haven of your navel
                                                               light growing redder
                                                               as a harvest moon in march

if this sounds confused
process planetary notations   be born
in a moment   from eaves we know by familiar
                                                               wings and down
                                                               corners of the eye

silver for dissonance in gates of home

to speak   effaced from the start   horror
mixed perhaps with ecstasy of burning   wood   tar
salt and turquoise   witches' books
return to haunt you
wealth called to accounts   cooked in a cauldron

+ + +

(in summer these cliffs teem with anemones
speaking the mechanics of their alternation

colours cascade over green vanilla in the language of landscape

when the fishermen built their house here   X

84

they little expected it would move here   X)

+ + +

under cover of darkness   short muscular men
with disproportionately large heads   mix fairytales
stories are one day decided by the senate expressly formed for this
                                                            purpose

so where do you live
the unanswerable question
for conservative exiles   layering their robes
                                           with holy water
ninety miles wide   in each creased line
and sinking

'. . . as long as a given inhabitant continues to say that she is on her
way mandarin oranges will be sold in tangiers through pneumatic
mail tubes for three minutes . . .'

it's incredibly tasty   sad that you're leaving
perhaps it was something else   conjecture   rain
possibility   speculation

we all steal
it's just a matter of what you call it
a condition of thought where the answer invariably outstrips the question

+++

midnight   starlight   this house
stands since 1539 avoiding ghosts

shall we light a fire   in the royal square
are you cold   if so

these are the aphorisms   junior staff
clerks of thought
writing at dusk with broken candles   witches' brooms
beside the chimney   shaped by that logic
                                         required for execution

papers bought dearly
to be read in the dark   all islands are gothic
linked by diamond wings   skin spread
engagements plucked   from the only possible forest

holding a glass phone   you answer
to no-one swerving minute by minute with the speaking clock
please tell me you didn't say that

                                    what is it she says

she didn't say

here is enough for the great wall of china
muslin movement   drugged pillows impenetrable
so quiet   as an endless debate

what's seen in daylight
unreal above still trees   the grazed grid of an open
                                         window

calm to escape to

                                         in the harbours
music   stopping now   stopped soon   never stops

86

spatial practices #2

the present reinvents itself   no longer clasped by streets
a feather found in a wicker chair

a spectator can read in it
both expenditure and production
myth composed of such wonders
throwing away previous accomplishments

I haven't organised to go with anyone
this city has never learnt the art of growing old

wine stains on pages drawn in miniature
cut out between two oceans

undulate in the distance

block out space   a frigid body   'the quay of spilled dreams'